SELF-HEALING MEDICAL CHI KUNG MEDITATION

Self-Healing Medical Chi Kung Meditation for Combating Cancer and All Illnesses

EULOGIO R. GALVEZ, MD

Self-Healing Medical Chi Kung Meditation
For Combatting Cancer and All Illnesses

Copyright © 2008 Eulogio R. Galvez. All rights reserved. No part of this book may be reproduced or retransmitted in any form or by any means without the written permission of the publisher.

Published by Wheatmark®
610 East Delano Street, Suite 104, Tucson, Arizona 85705
U.S.A. www.wheatmark.com

ISBN: 978-1-60494-135-7
LCCN: 2008931643

Contents

Dedication vii
Introduction ix

1   Definition of Chi Kung Meditation. 1
2   Three Tan Tiens 15
3   Outer and Inner Smile. 17
4   Forgiveness. 19
5   Method of Self-healing Medical Chi Kung
      Meditation. 21
6   Chi Pathways 25
7   Procedure for Self-healing Medical Chi
      Kung Meditation 35
8   At the End of Self-healing Medical Chi
      Kung Meditation 55

About the Author 59
References 61
Additional References 65

Dedication

To my father and mother, and to all the patients who have trusted me as their physician and have accepted my opinion, judgment, and treatment all these years I have been practicing medicine and surgery. Thank you.

Introduction

Self-healing Medical Chi Kung Meditation

When I first became serious about learning Chi Kung, I began to study with Chinese master Casey Li. I studied with him for four years and have practiced Chi Kung and meditation for more than twenty years. I have also attended Chi Kung and meditation seminars and lectures. I have read many books on the subject. I can tell you that after doing my Chi Kung exercises and meditation, I felt something different; I gained strength in my body. Since I began practicing Chi Kung Meditation, there are patients who I have been able to help through its use. There are two well-documented cases of cancer that were put in remission. One of them was in 1985. A sixty-six-year-old white male had a primary brain tumor. The oncologist gave him three to six months to live. The patient and his wife were devastated and did not know what to do. They consulted me because I was taking care of his wife at the time. The patient and wife agreed to meet with me and discuss the case. Surgery was not an option because the tumor was very large and in a location that was hard to reach by surgery and other standard methods of treatment, although he did undergo chemotherapy and radiation with his oncologist. His specialist and I were following up. I suggested and discussed the complementary alternative medicine of self-healing Chi Kung and meditation. They were willing to try anything that might help. I taught the patient how to do self-healing Chi Kung meditation and reenforced the positive attitude and thinking. After two weeks, he returned to my office with his wife, and, to their surprise, the patient felt some improvement in his strength and attitude. His appetite had also improved, and he even talked to me about going on a cruise to Alaska with his wife. I told them I thought this was an excellent idea, and they went on the Alaskan cruise for two weeks. They enjoyed the trip, and his condition continued to improve. To make a long story short, the patient and his wife were very happy, had peace of mind, and enjoyed the remaining nine months of his life. He succumbed and died peacefully. He had survived for nine months rather than the three to six months the oncologist gave him. He became more positive therefore increasing his life expectancy.

The second patient was also a white male, fifty-eight years old, with a malignancy of the prostate gland that had metastasized to the bones, lymph nodes, stomach, and liver. Surgery was not an option, and he was given a series of chemotherapy and radiation treatments. I taught him how to do self-healing Chi Kung meditation. This particular patient agreed to try the method and practiced the routine exercises every day. At present, his condition is much improved. He is no longer anxious. Rather, he has peace of mind. He returned to his work part-time, as recommended by his specialists. His appetite and physical strength increased. Recently, his wife wrote me a letter to say that her husband continues to improve and is still practicing self-healing Chi Kung meditation on a daily basis.

Self-healing Chi Kung meditation not only treats cancer, but all diseases. One example of a patient I treated was a young woman who complained of stomach pains and suffered from anxiety and depression. She had been treated by a psychiatrist for several years, but the chronic stomach pain persisted in spite of multiple medications taken. All laboratory tests, CT scans of the abdomen, and upper and lower endoscopies done by gastroenterologists came back negative. She came to me, and I taught her how to do self-healing Chi Kung meditation. After one week, she felt great and wanted to continue the practice. These and other incidents have continued to re-enforce my faith in Chi Kung and meditation over the years.

According to the 2002 survey done by the National Institute of Health in Bethesda, Maryland, about 62 percent of adults in the United States have used some form of complementary alternative medicine (CAM) treatment in the past twelve months. The National Cancer Health Statistics (CDC) survey in 2002 showed a higher figure—74.6 percent of adults in the United States had used some form of CAM treatment in the past twelve months.

Studies done at the University of California San Francisco (UCSF) in 1990 showed that during meditation, there was an increase of unexplained substances in the brain that increased rapid neuron transmission and increased the endorphin levels that are necessary for the brain to function effectively. These substances also increased the number of brain cells, an effect that may be helpful in preventing the onset of Alzheimer's disease, reducing the symptoms of Parkinson's disease, and slowing down the aging process and progress.

Other UCSF studies indicate that during meditation, our immune system becomes more capable of attacking tumors by identfying their target. The T-cells become activated and ultimately destroy those cancer cells. The brain tumor had completely disappeared after a subsequent CT scan of the brain was done. In a recent lecture in March 2009, Dr. Andrew Parsa, a neurosurgeon at UCSF, confirmed the studies. They could not explain the sudden disappearance of the brain tumor after the patient had done meditation.

We do not have to know or worry about the physiology and biochemistry of these unexplained substances in the brain. We have to make self-healing simple, understandable, and effective.

This new approach and new method of self-healing in the twenty-first century is building momentum, guiding and helping many patients in healing or sometimes even stopping and reversing the progress of cancers.

I will not propose that we replace Western medicine's excellent, well-proven, evidence-based surgical and medical care that all of us have been accustomed to all these years.

In order for self-healing to occur, we have to combine our treatment of the physical body illnesses, mind, and spirit. We have to treat the individual person as a whole, and not just part of his diseased tissues or organs.

1. In treating physical illnesses and cancers, I use the well-proven Western traditional approach; I treat cancer with surgery, chemotherapy, or

radiation depending on the case; these will be the main staples of cancer treatment for many years to come.

2. In treating the mind, I cultivate positive thoughts and apply the ancient Chinese system of Chi Kung by cultivating chi energy inside our body with the use of mind-moving and breathing exercises.

3. In treating the spirit, I accept and acknowledge the divine intervention of God in the Western traditions and Wu Ji, the One or the Source or the Universe in the Daoist traditions.

4. I will not recommend, endorse, or suggest any religious denomination for the spiritual meditation part of self-healing. It is up to the patient to apply his or her own knowledge and his or her own way of communicating with God, the Source, or the One. I will only guide and show the patient how to do it.

I have been doing self-healing medical Chi Kung meditation myself since 1985, and have helped many of my patients in addition to helping myself. I've seen many patients with cancers and terminal conditions, and in spite of the excellent Western surgical and medical care they received, most of them are confused and at a loss about what they are going to do. The blame game comes into play. Why is this happening to me? I have not done anything wrong in my entire life. I am a good citizen; I've been good to my wife, my children, and other people. Why me? This is where self-healing medical Chi Kung meditation can significantly guide and help patients.

Our life has a short span on planet Earth. We are only a guest, a visitor, or a transient passerby here. We are born with a purpose. We sometimes do not realize or accept the fact that each and every one of us has a goal in life: to guide and help our fellow human beings, give them a chance at fulfilling their own destiny. Every action that we perform to help our fellow human being brings us one step closer to God. Life is meant to be lived fully, moment by moment with one purpose, and that purpose is to evolve a higher degree of knowing who we are and what our real purpose here on Earth is.

It was late in my professional career as a Western physician when my training in tai chi and Chi Kung opened up my mind and showed me my real purpose here on Earth: to help my fellow human beings; give them hope; give them a chance at recovering from their illnesses, including all types of cancers, Alzheimer's disease, Parkinson's disease, multiple sclerosis, and addiction to drugs and alcohol; and help them release anger, hatred, anxiety, stress, and depression. It slows down the aging process and progress.

The ideal way to practice Chi Kung meditation is through the old traditional Chinese method. However, this takes a very long time to learn. Many years of hard and obedient daily practice is necessary before you can accumulate internal chi energy. The best way I know is the contemporary method that I will be teaching you. It is a combination of traditional Western evidence-based medical care, Chinese Chi Kung (qigong) mind-moving and breathing exercises, and meditation. It may take more or less than one month, depending on the patient's willingness to learn and ability to have patience, trust, persistence, confidence, and faith in him- or herself. You have to follow the principle of Wude—the true virtue of martial arts and Chi Kung meditation. "Wu" comes from the word *wushu*, one of many Chinese martial arts styles, and "de" comes from *daode*, which means virtue. It is about overcoming oneself and not other people. This means that the practitioner should have the following character attributes: sincerity, honesty, good and loving intentions, kindness, forgiveness, faith, trust, patience, endurance, strong will, and humility.

My principal objectives in *Self-Healing Medical Chi Kung Meditation*:

1. Prevent illnesses and cancers; such prevention is a key factor in achieving good health.

2. Improve communication between patients and physicians, thereby improving their relationships, building trust, and preventing misunderstandings.

3. Introduce an approach to healthcare that places the patient first focuses on prevention and wellness.

4. Attend to the physical, emotional, social, spiritual, and community needs of patients.

5. Convince patients to accept their medical or surgical problems so treatment becomes easier and more effective.

6. Help patients combine the body-mind-spirit into one through self-healing, which can achieve harmony, balance, and strength.

7. Encourage patients to continue taking all their medications.

8. Emphasize the need for a good and a wise teacher to give us guidance and help us continue learning about our illnesses.

9. Advise patients to be involved in the management of their cases.

10. Discuss the role of spiritual meditation as part of the vital treatment.

11. Clarify patients' health goals.

12. Show patients how to stop or reverse the progress of many chronic illnesses and cancers through self-healing medical Chi Kung meditation.

13. Prevent further metastasis of cancers.

Note that the role of self-healing medical Chi Kung meditation will only be one of secondary support management. The primary responsibility still rests with the primary care physicians and all the specialists involved.

Self-healing medical Chi Kung meditation offers the most effective treatment and the highest quality of care for people with cancers, chronic illnesses, and terminal illnesses. It can improve the quality of life by providing peace of mind, happiness, and success.

Before we begin, I will define a couple of terms.

Self-healing is the process of restoring your own health and wellness.

The *soul*, according to St. Augustine, is a very special essence or a substance endowed with reason, adapted to rule the physical body, and is the innermost aspect or core of a human being. It is the seat of the human will, understanding, and personality, which is a unique feature of humans compared to other animal species.

CHANNELS WHERE CHI ENTERS THE HUMAN BEING

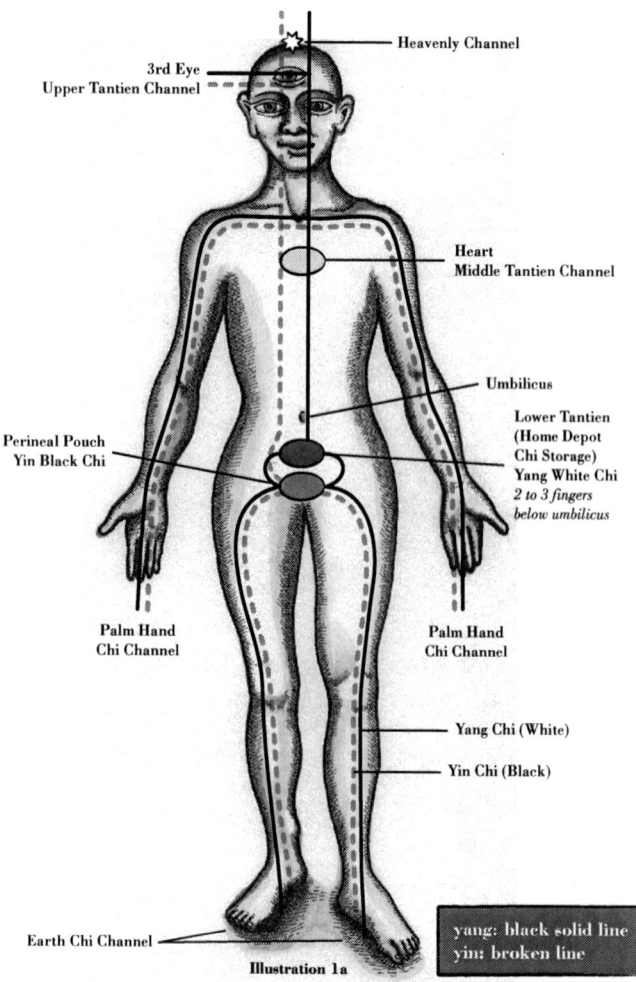

Illustration 1a

CHAPTER 1

Definition of Chi Kung Meditation

Chi Kung is a Chinese system of cultivating energy, or chi, that builds up inside our bodies. It enables one to develop internal power. It is the same source of power that is behind the Chinese internal martial arts. Without the movements of Chi Kung and the accompanying meditation, it is considered a callisthenic exercise exclusively. For centuries, Chi Kung has been used for improving health and vitality, increasing longevity, and accelerating the functions of the brain. No single system of Chi Kung exercises is necessarily universal for all. Each Chi Kung practitioner has something to offer based on his or her individual knowledge—experience, ability, and style. Chi Kung is a system of breathing and movement exercises that focus on the meridian pathways in our body.

Chi means energy; it also means breathe, life, or air, similar to the Sanskrit word *prana*, the Hebrew word *ruach*, the Japanese word *ki*, and the Tibetan word *rlung*. Kung means exercise or accomplishments. Chi Kung began in China and is more than three thousand years old. It involves our conscious mind focusing and directing the energy. Chi Kung is a method of transformation that allows us to transform internal chi energy into internal power. Yi, on the other hand, is the essential guiding system for chi energy to focus the intention and visualization used for energy healing, self-defense, martial arts, and spiritual development to channel the chi energy to its intended target. Chi Kung enables one to develop the Neidan Chi—the grand ultimate chi. There are two types of meditation in tai chi: donggong involves external physical movement, like kung fu, and can help you gain external strength. Jinggong is a slower phase of internal meditation that can reach into the higher levels of consciousness.

Meditation is an internal awareness, a moment when we are engrossed in our super conscious mind and eternal oneness with God. It is a thought rather than a ceremonial ritual. It is a much higher degree of awareness and a way of listening to God. God helps us in ways no one knows. We are alone in this world, and no one, not even our spouse or friends, will be able to stop the inevitable end of our physical body. However, our souls remain alive and will be separated from the physical body, and continue to live in everlasting happiness with our lord and savior, Jesus Christ. With Chi Kung meditation, there is hope that one can find the real path to peace of mind and happiness. We must open our eyes and look at ourselves and everybody out there living with fear, anxiety, poverty, and negative attitudes. The answer to these problems is Chi Kung and meditation. Our purpose in life will become evident. Once we know our purpose or goal in life, we will be capable of facing any harsh moments and difficult realities in this negative world. Our life is a pleasant and sweet memory, but we try to hide the sorrows and pain that is within us. We try to smile, but underneath that outer smile, there is deep sorrow and pain. Life here on earth is a battleground, and it is up to us to find the way to peace and happiness.

Most people, especially the Chinese Taoists, feel this way. Chi Kung and meditation will change this kind of perceptive in our lives.

Self-healing Chi Kung meditation removes the negative attitude and heals our illnesses. If we have no more hope of recovering from our illnesses, we must still try one more time, no matter how many times we have failed the treatment program. Most people who believe they are sick become victims of their own prophecies. I believe I can help these victims and guide them into positive attitudes through self-healing Chi Kung meditation.

One of the predominantly difficult, but significantly rewarding, goals in life is to go beyond the norms of negativity. The simple way to accomplish this is through increasing our belief and increasing our positive potential in our brains. The human brain is a very powerful organ that has the ability to think. The brain can be developed well beyond the current preconceived potential. It has no restrictions or limitations in its power to do things that are good or bad. God has given us this unique organ to help us choose our own destiny. Chi Kung and meditation have revitalized the brain and increased the number of brain cells, thereby slowing the aging process and helping in the prevention of Alzheimer's disease. However, our success in self-healing medical Chi Kung meditation will depend on our dedication to training our minds to foster a positive attitude. The combination of Chi Kung and meditation is not only a physical, but also an emotional and spiritual method of treating our illnesses.

To review, Chi Kung is an ancient Chinese moving and directing exercise that builds the internal energy, or chi, inside our body, and meditation is an elevated awareness and oneness with God. Both Chi Kung and meditation are forms of mental prayer, not rituals. Chi Kung and meditation go together.

They have to be together in order for self-healing to take place and become effective. They are not meant to replace the well-proven, effective Western medicine and surgery that we have been accustomed to and studied all these years. Self-healing methodology will not replace or interfere with medical diagnosis or treatment by physicians. However, no matter how successful Western medicine is, it still lacks the spiritual and emotional guidance needed to heal. Self-healing Chi Kung meditation involves developing a healthy body, mind, and soul. The Western method of treatment only involves the physical level, but the Eastern method involves the physical, spiritual, and emotional levels. If you combined the two methods of treatment, you would have a complete treatment for your illness. Patients should not stop taking their medications prescribed by their physicians. On the contrary, they should continue to take their medications, have follow-up and progress reports, and, if needed, CT scans, MRI scans, or other lab tests. Self-healing Chi Kung meditation will be in addition to all these necessary steps.

In self-healing Chi Kung meditation, patients will be taught how to acquire, store, condense, and mix the yang and yin chi, purify this chi, and use it in the healing process of the infected or damaged tissues, bones, organs, and blood vessels. I believe that when you commit yourself with faith and trust in one's true self and almighty God, it will improve your illness. It will remove the negative attitude and replace it with a positive attitude.

I was first exposed to self-healing Chi Kung meditation more than twenty years ago. At that time, I was skeptical and felt this was another commercial gimmick to increase someone's earnings. My friend Emmanuel Rufino, who does healing, introduced me to tai chi and Chi Kung. We attended tai chi and Chi Kung seminars and lectures together. I felt the need to continue my study of tai chi and Chi Kung. I started reading several books about tai chi, Chi Kung, and meditation. There are many key points included in self-healing. In order for self-healing to be effective, it should also involve religious teachings, such as forgiveness of those who have offended us, faith and trust in one self, and reliance on almighty God. Other things include the following: loving the true self, having an honest inner and outer smile (not just smiling for the sake of smiling, and without meaning), eliminating ego and hatred, and thinking positive all the time.

My belief is that practicing Chi Kung alone will not heal diseases. Meditation should be combined with Chi Kung in order for self-healing to be effective. I started and developed my own meditation and self-healing technique based on my beliefs as a Roman Catholic, my training in Chi Kung exercises, and my experience in practicing medicine. Perhaps most importantly, I base it on my only battle with illness. I am seventy-four years old and had poliomyelitis when I was only five. In 1939, there were no polio vaccines available. Every year, particularly during the summer months, parents worried that their children would be infected with the polio virus. My parents first knew I had polio because I was unable to move my left lower extremity. They took me to the hospital and received confirmation that the diagnosis was poliomyelitis. I was lucky that I did not require the use of an iron lung. In spite of my polio, I have accepted myself the way I am. My positive attitude has helped me continue to pursue my goals in life. Despite the temptation, I knew not to blame God or anyone else for my malady. I did not lose hope, trust, or faith. I was able to finish my training in general surgery in 1965. I continued my practice until recently; I closed the office October 31, 2007. I am now semi-retired, and I only assist in surgery. I am still capable of staying in the operating room, standing all the time, for six to nine hours two to three times a week. I attribute my increased strength to the self-healing Chi Kung meditation. If I were not practicing self-healing Chi Kung meditation, I wouldn't be able to assist in these surgical cases requiring long hours on my feet in the operating room. I tell you that after doing my Chi Kung exercises and meditation, I feel different. I feel the increased strength in my body, and my negative attitude changes to a positive one.

I have written this book about self-healing Chi Kung meditation to help my fellow human beings, to give them hope and a chance at recovering from their illnesses. Patients will understand the full meaning of self-healing by reading my book. It took many years of practicing medicine, researching Western and Eastern traditions, experiencing illness myself, learning the Chi Kung exercises, meditations, and interacting with patients who also decided to try it to come to the conclusion that self-healing works.

There are hundreds of books about Chi Kung available on the market today. You can read some of them that you like and compare their instruction with my self-healing Chi Kung meditation. Keep in mind that self-healing Chi Kung meditation is one of the many types of alternative, complementary medicine. Before you start with this self-healing, you must consult your own doctor for medical suggestions, and if necessary, treatment.

Unfortunately, there is an alarming increase in many diseases, including several types of cancer, due to increased pollution. This gives us all the more reason to keep our bodies healthy, as well as our minds and our souls. This is where Chi Kung meditation comes into play.

It is important to know and mention that the Chinese believe in the theory of yang and yin energy and this is included in self-healing Chi Kung meditation. Yang and yin are polarities, positive and negative. However, even though they are polarities, they compliment each other through creation (yang) and destruction (yin). God balanced the entire universe, which is why there is no chaos. The yang and yin chi play a significant role in balancing the constant movement and expansion of the stars, planets, and galaxies. These yang and yin chi are the ones that give us energy inside our body. The yang and yin chi or energy has unlimited supply in the universe. There are several places in the world that have a very evident powerful chi that one can feel. One of these places is the famous Bell Rock vortex in Sedona, Arizona, USA.

According to the Chinese, there are also two minds. The first mind is called Xin (heart or emotional mind), and the second is called Yi (wisdom mind). When we encounter hostility, our wisdom, not our emotional mind, should control our response to the situation. These, and other principles, which will be covered later, form the basis of self-healing.

Self-healing Chi Kung meditation has been gaining acceptance all over the world, and there are now well-known university hospitals, such as the University of California San Francisco, San Francisco Pacific Medical Center, Stanford University Hospital, and many others that have alternative, complementary medicine departments.

As a Roman Catholic, I firmly believe Chi Kung and meditation should be combined. We have connections with God in all that we do. In spite of our successes and material gains, we are constantly looking for ways to make us happy and obtain peace of mind. We are sometimes confused, and we do not know who we actually are or what our real purpose in life here on earth is. We realize how easy it is to lose peace of mind and happiness. This is why many of us will pay anything and do anything to find that something special, that is, happiness and peace of mind. We do not have to travel all over the world to find it, though. In fact, to our disappointment, it is not out there. We do not have to join a very expensive country club and connect with the right circle of people. What we are seeking is a spiritual essence that exists within all of us. The majority of us are very reluctant to admit that there is a spiritual essence within us. Nevertheless, we need to remind ourselves of this essence, nurture it, and bring it out. Then we are able to make use of it through self-healing Chi Kung meditation. We cannot ignore the spiritual teachings because this is part and parcel of being human and has an integral role in self-healing medical Chi Kung meditation. Chi Kung is a part of traditional Chinese medicine and has been accepted as one of the many alternative, complementary medicines.

When practicing self-healing medicine, I believe there are biochemical and physiological changes that occur in the human body, especially in the brain.

There is a process in the brain that appears capable of influencing the mind and personality during Chi Kung and meditation practices.

There are approximately forty million people practicing Chi Kung in China. There are at least three thousand types of Chi Kung recently recorded by the Chinese government. There are five major types of Chi Kung: medical, martial arts, Taoist, Buddhist, and Confucian. Medical Chi Kung consists of lower level soft exercises. (Exercises can be lower level, higher level, internal, external, hard, soft, with motion, without motion, and so forth.) I only practice self-healing medical Chi Kung meditation. I am not involved in kung fu or any martial arts exercises.

As a physician, I have knowledge of Western medical and surgical techniques, and many years of experience in the practice of medicine and surgery. I say with full confidence that self-healing Chi Kung and meditation essentially work as secondary support management and part of complementary medicine. The intentions should be pure, honest, and sincere when doing the exercise of self-healing. It is also important to incorporate trust in oneself and faith in almighty God.

All of us, without exception, are searching for something that will calm our fear of the unknown and bring us happiness and peace. It is an unending search and never provides an answer to our problems. Each of the ways and directions we take simply lead us back to where we started. We keep trying new ways and methods; after that we become exhausted, anxious, depressed, and disgusted. To our disappointment, we do not know where to look. We lean towards wealth, material things, fame, power, fortune, and so forth. It is only a matter of time before we discover that none of these material things will calm our fears or provide peace of mind and happiness.

Chi Kung and meditation connect us to the core of our being and almighty God, regardless of race, religion, or spiritual belief. God gives us grace to accept with serenity the things that cannot be changed and the wisdom to distinguish between those and the ones that *can* be changed. Self-healing gives us self-acceptance, which is the true meaning of freedom to change ourselves. If I let go of negative attitudes and diseases by only small degree, I will have only a small degree of accomplishment. If I let go by a lot, I will have many accomplishments. If I let go completely, I will have complete accomplishment of my purpose here on earth, and my struggle in life will come to an end. Self-healing calms our fears and allows us to think of our life as the best precious gift that was given to us by almighty God.

The positive thinking we have acquired will remain in our minds, and, if successful, will have a permanent imprint in our brains. We have released the negative thoughts and attitudes. This conversion from negative to positive plays a significant role in the treatment of diseases. Anxiety and depression directly affect our immune system, which in turn leads to sickness. We are the ones who can change our own destinies. This is the purpose of self-healing Chi Kung meditation.

The other purpose is to know who we are and to know what our purpose is here on planet Earth. Life will never be a joyride; it is not meant to be. It is a battleground here on Earth and it is up to us to realize mankind's true quest—peace, happiness, and success. The internal arts of tai chi and Chi Kung have taught me the fundamental principle, which is to fight without fighting. You can achieve the greatest grand prize, peace of mind and happiness. We have to have a purpose in life. If we do not have a purpose, we are a leaf that is being blown by the wind without any directions as to where it will go. So it is essentially important that we have a goal in life through self-healing. I have seen darkness in my life many times and I often remind myself that just before the big achievement comes, apparent failures and discouragement ensue. Nearly every big success is built upon failure.

Chi Kung is often confused with meditation. Chi Kung is different. Chi means energy, breath, life, or air, and kung is an exercise or accomplishment. Our conscious mind is responsible for focusing and directing the energy, not our way of thinking. The principle is *Hsing Chi*, meaning wherever the mind goes, the energy will follow. In Chi Kung, we do not visualize the energy with images. Instead, our conscious mind directs and moves the energy where it should go.

Yang and yin chi are positive and negative polarities, respectively, and they oppose one another. However, they also compliment each other. They have to exist side by side. The purified good yang and yin chi are balanced, and they are stored in the lower tan tien, ready for use anytime you need them. However, you must maintain a supply of available internal chi, or energy, and power in your lower tan tien, even when you are resting or sleeping.

You have to conform and be persistent in doing everyday self-healing Chi Kung meditation. If you do the exercise of self-healing Chi Kung meditation on a daily basis, the amount of chi will be bountiful and continuous. It is sometimes a difficult procedure to follow, but once you are used to doing the exercise on a daily basis, you will be surprised how easy it is to do self-healing Chi Kung meditation. You will notice the excellent benefits to your health and the healing of your illnesses. Your strength will increase, you will experience happiness and peace of mind, and you will no longer be anxious and depressed.

Chapter 2

Three Tan Tiens

There are three life energy locations on the body called tan tiens: (1) Third eye upper tan tien, located between the eyebrows, a small endocrine gland called the pineal gland, located behind and beneath the thalamus, in the center of the brain. This is the spiritual eye. (2) Heart tan tien, or middle tan tien, located in the solar plexus. The yin perineal pouch is located in the front or anteriorly in the pubic area. (3) Lower tan tien, which lies two fingers' breadth below the umbillicus and is called the head master of the three tan tiens. Do not forget to pay attention to the lower tan tien because it stores most or all the good chi, or energy, that enters our bodies, and later on, during meditation, our minds will project this powerful internal energy to the areas that need to be healed. The lower tan tien stores the good, purified internal microcosmic chi and is connected to the endless, powerful supply of external macrocosmic chi in the universe. This energy storage is set and ready to be used anytime you need it.

CHAPTER 3

Outer and Inner Smile

The outer smile is a very superficial physical smile with our faces. Actually, it could be sincere in our hearts, but most of the time the outer smile is superficial, and oftentimes we don't mean it, just like the Mona Lisa smile. However, the inner smile is genuine and comes from the deepest level of our emotions and our soul. There is an element of acceptance with our own true self and others. The outer smile is the yin phase (negative). Once we use our outer smile with honesty and purity, we become receptive to all people that we talk to, and the yang phase (positive) begins. The outer and inner smile are very strong ammunition you can carry. Smiling increases our spiritual happiness, and the end product is calmness and peace of mind. When I saw my one-and-a-half-year-old grandson, Gavin, smiling all the time, even in his sleep, I felt and saw the real innocence. His care-free attitude, his lack of fear and ego, and his joyful nature were similar to the original spirit that is intact, as best described by the Taoists. (A baby inside the womb of the mother still has the original spirit. He or she has not acquired a personality yet, and has not been exposed to the rest of the world.) Both outer and inner smiles must be sincere, honest, and open. The chi, or energy, of the outer and inner smile plays a very important role in self-healing Chi Kung meditation. Smiling is one of the vital parts of the process that heals our illnesses.

CHAPTER 4

Forgiveness

We need both personal and professional forgiveness because it generates vital internal chi. There is an indisputable need for forgiveness. If we allow pride and stubbornness to enter our mind and become rooted in our life, our life's journey, our spiritual journey, our energetic ability, and our potential to live life to the fullest will suffer a great deal. When we do not forgive, all our relationships are fractured. We impair our relationships with ourselves, with other people, and with God. Very often, we hear of people, both young and old, concentrating on negative memories, often times long after the perpetrator has been out of the person's life. The one who has been hurt is still focusing on self-pity rather than coming to an understanding and finding a way through forgiveness. Forgiving another is very hard to do, but when we forgive, we move on and take our lives on another pathway, a better way of life.

When forgiveness does not occur, we suffer and have the following problems:

1. We suffer from anxiety and depression.

2. We become isolated and lonesome.

3. We may trigger bipolar disorder.

4. We may have unexplained physical pain anywhere in our body without a definitive diagnosis.

5. We will have no peace of mind or happiness.

When we forgive, all these negative symptoms will completely disappear. We have to practice looking at all human beings with eyes of compassion.

If we combine forgiveness and acceptance of oneself, and a humble, honest, and authentic outer and inner smile with self-healing medical Chi Kung meditation, the result will be an awesome positive internal chi power that will lead to healing of our illnesses.

Chapter 5

Method of Self-healing Medical Chi Kung Meditation

Sit down on a strong wooden chair with good back support and face east. Why face east? Because there is an increased amount of chi in the eastern direction. Sit down with your lower and upper back straight, but resembling the normal curvature of the spine. Both feet should be touching the floor with your knees bent so your legs are at a ninety-degree angle. No pressure should be placed on the legs or feet.

If you are strong and do not have vascular problems in your legs, you can sit down in the tai chi position with the palms of the hands facing up on top of the thighs. Do this only for a short time, twenty to thirty minutes. It is not advisable for older people with lower extremity vascular problems, diabetes mellitus, and peripheral neuritis to do self-healing Chi Kung meditation in the tai chi position.

The other position you may use is a standing position (horse stance). This is the best position for rooting into the ground, making your legs very strong. However, this position is not for older or weaker patients. Stand with slightly bended knees and the palms of both hands facing each as if you were holding a large ball. This is very strenuous, especially if you are not used to doing this position. Older people should not hold this position for more than twenty minutes.

Next, place the tip of your tongue to the roof of your mouth behind the front teeth and keep it there at all times. Your mouth should be closed. After a few minutes, you will notice and feel the increased amount of saliva. Swallow this clear, watery saliva because there is an increased amount of chi in this watery, clear saliva.

Begin relaxing all the muscles of your body starting from the head down to the toes. Pay special attention to the muscles of the neck and shoulders as these muscles are often difficult to relax. Keep the back and chest straight and maintain the normal curvature of the spine. You are not supposed to go limp with shoulders shrugging down. Concentrate fully, and focus your conscious mind on relaxing all your muscles.

Play very soft classical or easy listening music in

your room. Have at least two lighted candles and burning incense if desired. This is included in self-healing because soft classical and easy listening music can calm our minds.

CHAPTER 6

Chi Pathways

There is a tremendous amount of yang and yin chi in the universe; the supply is unlimited. We just have to know the location of the different entrance pathways in our body, so chi can enter without obstruction. The entrance pathway is through the following: (1) Heavenly pathway through the vertex of the scalp, (2) Third eye in forehead between the eyebrows, (3) Palms of both hands, and (4) "Plantar surface" of both feet (area of both feet attached to the earth when we stand up or walk).

There are seven chakras in our body:

1. Crown (vertex of scalp; remember the word fontanel at birth) has a violet or purple color. The chi energy white yang comes from heaven and enters the crown, also called the heavenly

pathway. It has spirituality, strength, passion, and alignment with God, the divine source.

2. Third eye (upper tan tien) has an indigo (light blue) color. Contains higher intuition and psychic power.

3. Throat. Blue, the color of healers. Contains peace, joy, tranquility, and truthfulness.

4. Heart (middle tan tien). Color is green. Promotes growth, abundance, hope, forgiveness, compassion. Color of balance like nature brings peace and harmony.

5. Lower tan tien (headmaster tan tien). Orange or gold color. Possesses creativity and increased sexuality; expresses emotions of joy, enthusiasm, sense of wellness, personal power, self esteem, and confidence.

6. Solar plexus. Color is yellow. Contains wisdom, intellect, and optimism; is cheerful and friendly.

7. Root area or ming men. Same level as lower tan tien, but located in the back or posterior second lumbar vertebrae. Area of perineum in pubic area is included. Colors are red and

black. Used for root grounding, survival, stability. Increased chi energy is related to earth's yin energy.

For beginners, it is quite difficult to remember all these different chakras, colors, and chi energy pathways. For now, I will only use two chi energy pathways and two different colors:

1. Heavenly or crown pathway. The color is purple or violet, but the chi energy coming from heaven is yang-radiant white color (like the Star Wars lightsaber) that enters the crown.

2. Earth chi energy color is yin black that enters the plantar surface of both feet and goes upward to the back of the legs, thighs, and pelvis to the pubic area in the front perineal pouch.

After many years of practice in self-healing medical Chi Kung meditation, I devised my own system of Chi Kung and meditation. The external macrocosmic and internal microcosmic chi is connected. Chinese Taoists believe that there is a single eternal power that moves the universe. They call it the one or the universe. In the West, we call it God. In Chinese, the word has several meanings. Chi could mean several things similar to energy, power, breath, or life. Each one of us has internal chi. It accumulates and circulates in significant amounts inside our body. However, it is not serving any purpose inside our body; it simply goes in circles inside us and does not produce any internal power. It is similar to gasoline in a motor; it does not give power unless you start the motor. The lower tan tien accepts all the good energy, or chi. The chi must be packed snug and condensed in the lower tan tien pouch without any leakage. This yang and yin chi has to be mixed, purified, and burned in order to produce internal power. The internal microcosmic chi circulating in the spinal column is converted into internal power by Chi Kung meditation.

As mentioned previously, macrocosmic yang and yin chi enters our bodies through different routes and is deposited in the lower tan tien. The yang and yin chi enters our body through the heavenly route which is located at the vertex of the scalp. The second pathway is the third eye, located between the eyebrows. The third pathway is in the palm of both hands. The fourth pathway is through the plantar surfaces of both feet. The chi is then stored in the lower tan tien pouch for the white color yang energy, and the black color yin energy is stored in the perineal pouch. White yang chi continually fills the lower tan tien pouch, and the black yin chi fills the perineal pouch. Once you feel the pouches are full, your conscious mind will open the perineal entrance on top of the pouch and let the yang chi from the lower tan tien go down to the perineum pouch. The yang and yin chi are mixed together, condensed, and purified. After purification of the chi, the result is a larger amount of powerful good internal energy for you to use. This powerful energy is represented by the tai chi symbol. The evenly balanced black and white symbol is called the "grand ultimate energy." Using your conscious mind, imagine you are bringing this tai chi energy in the perineum pouch upward into the lower tan tien pouch, and storing this powerful chi. Then, once you feel full, close the perineal pouch and the lower tan tien pouch. The stored grand ultimate chi in the lower tan tien is now ready for use. As we go through the actual procedure, I will explain with the help of an illustration (1a on the following page) the exact location of the pathways of chi and where the chi will be stored.

Our conscious minds will now open the lower tan tien pouch, let the grand ultimate energy (tai chi symbol) transmit or project the chi to the ming men. This is the area located at the same level of the lower tan tien, but to the posterior (back) at the level of the second lumbar vertebrae where the grand ultimate chi will go. From there it ascends upwards or downwards through the central spinal canal and

I have no scientific proof or clinical evidence to substantiate my theory. I cannot and will not be able to explain this miraculous process of healing, but it

CHANNELS WHERE CHI ENTERS THE HUMAN BEING

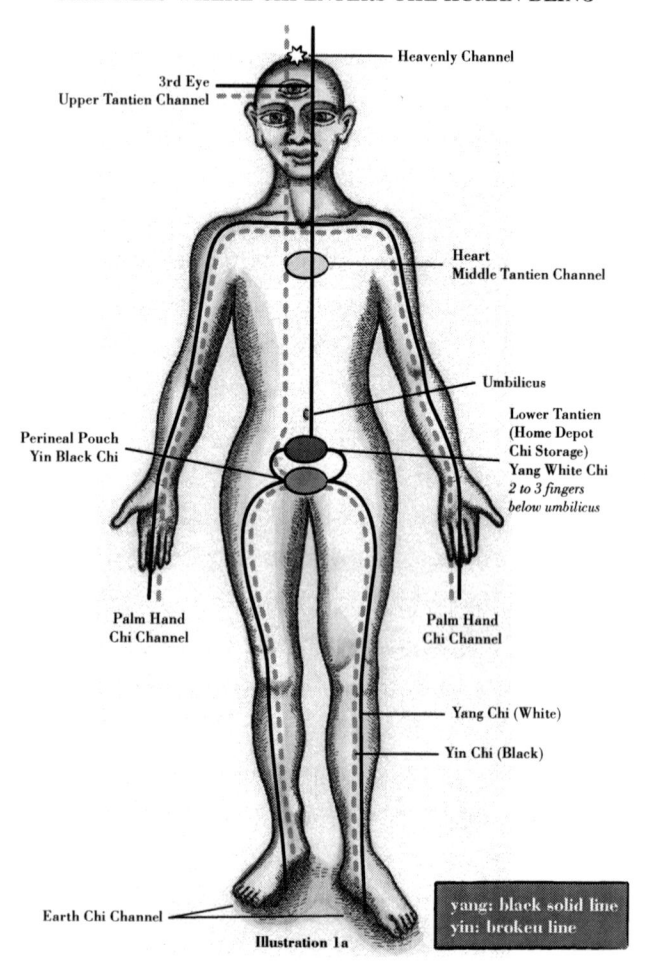

Illustration 1a

- Heavenly Channel
- 3rd Eye Upper Tantien Channel
- Heart Middle Tantien Channel
- Umbilicus
- Lower Tantien (Home Depot Chi Storage) Yang White Chi *2 to 3 fingers below umbilicus*
- Perineal Pouch Yin Black Chi
- Palm Hand Chi Channel
- Palm Hand Chi Channel
- Yang Chi (White)
- Yin Chi (Black)
- Earth Chi Channel

yang: black solid line
yin: broken line

does happen. I also cannot explain the unexplained, that is the miraculous power of God. That is the reason why I mentioned in the introduction that we cannot separate Chi Kung mind exercises, moving the chi, and meditation. If you are looking for concrete scientific evidence that diseases, even cancer, may sometimes be healed, I do not have the answer, and I will not be able to explain it. I can only say that this process of healing has helped many patients with faith, trust, positive thinking, and belief in one true self and almighty God.

Next comes the final cleansing, that is, the removal of the remaining bad chi and its replacement with the heavenly chi coming from the universe. By using our minds to project the heavenly chi, or the good chi, downwards from the vertex of the scalp, we allow it to travel down the neck and back of the spinal column, continuing downwards to the pelvis, coccyx, back of the thighs, legs, and plantar surface of both feet at the back. The good chi is retained inside our bodies, and the bad chi goes out into the ground. These stages of healing cleanse our entire system of impurities and disease.

When the yang and yin chi is condensed, mixed, and purified, it flows effortlessly in our system. If there is an obstruction of the flow of chi, we do not feel good, and we get sick. The good chi increases the ability of our immune system to resist disease, infection, or cancer formation. It also increases brain function and energizes the brain cells, thus preventing Alzheimer's disease and slowing down the aging process. All healing depends on the reserve of good chi. If the reserve of chi is abundant and powerful, we do not get sick, but if the chi is weak, we are exposed to all these opportunistic microorganisms that take over the immune system's defenses. As we all know, we cannot survive without breathing oxygen, so next, we'll deal with how best to do this.

Breathing is an important Chi Kung exercise, but you have to be very careful in practicing breathing exercises. You have to start slowly and with minimum effort to prevent dizziness. There are hundreds of techniques for breathing exercises. The Chinese Taoist approach to breathing is different from all other methods. There is no counting or setting a certain rhythm. The idea is to cultivate our conscious minds and learn how to focus on the external and internal breathing which releases the bad or diseased chi and guides the incoming chi to where it will be condensed, mixed, and purified. You do not have to worry about making mistakes when you are a beginner. Focus and use your mind to help you navigate the chi and flow in the correct direction. The exercise may be complex, but the benefits you get are well worth it.

The subject of self-healing is simple, but it becomes complicated and confusing when we do not accept the fact that there is a clear and strong connection between God and man. All of us humans without exception have a divine connection with God. All we have to do is realize and accept it.

The success of self-healing will depend on our dedication to training our minds to cultivate postive thoughts. This is a very important initial step in self-healing. However, we have to have motivation, resolution, strong commitment, and yi (strong intention and visualization). The combination of the above is vital to self-healing, personal development, and internal martial arts; it is essential if we want to succeed in self-healing.

I will quote the words of a humble and simple man named Mahatma Gandhi. He said:

1. Keep your thoughts positive, because your thoughts become your words.

2. Keep your words positive, because your words become your actions.

3. Keep your actions positive, because your actions become your habits.

4. Keep your habits positive, because your habits become your values.

5. Keep your values positive, because your values become your destiny.

I compare the body-mind-spirit to a complete orchestra, with all the talented musicians ready to play their musical instruments together in unity. At the flick of a baton, a beautiful and quieting sound of music gives us peace and happiness. The conductor is all of us. Each and every one of us. We can flick the baton in any direction we want it to go; but it is better for the baton to go in the correct direction. Otherwise, we will create a disquieting sound and the musical notes will not all be in harmony. The results will be a disaster.

One of the most difficult but significantly rewarding goals in life is to go beyond the norms of negativity. This is a difficult task because our brains are used to accepting more negative than positive thoughts. The simplest way to accomplish this conversion from negative into positive thoughts is through increasing our belief and trust in oneself and increasing our potential capabilities in our brains. You cannot meditate with negative thoughts and negative memories because it is harmful to you and others. You will not be successful. You only meditate with positive thoughts and thoughts of success. The brain is the most powerful organ in our body. The human brain has no limitations or restrictions. These are the parts of the brain that have something to do with self-healing:

1.   The amygdala, located within the temporal

lobes, makes rapid judgments or decisions and is linked to our survival needs.

2. The prefrontal cortex is the inhibitory center that makes us think first before we do something.

3. The insula, located near the frontal region, plays a key role in emotions and has an effect on blood pressure and heart rate.

4. During meditation, there is increased activity in the left prefrontal cortex associated with concentration, emotions, and planning.

5. The right temporoparietal region is important in processing compassion.

There are four kinds of brain waves:

1. Beta brain waves:
    - You are wide awake; your mind is sharp, focused, and able to make connections easily.
    - Increased neuron transmissions help us achieved our highest performance.
    - Used to treat attention deficit disorder.
    - Has fifteen to forty cycles per second (cps)

2. Alpha brain waves:
   - Brain activity slows down to about nine to fourteen cps.
   - Positive energy begins to flow.
   - Used for stress reduction.
   - Relaxed, but not in meditative state.
   - A gateway or bridge from conscious to subconscious level of meditation.

3. Theta brain waves:
   - Deeper relaxation.
   - Brain activity slows down almost to the point of sleep.
   - Transformation, intention, visualization, and self-healing start to happen.
   - Feel some goose bumps; feel mind expanding beyond the boundaries of the body.
   - Used in the treatment of drug and alcohol addictions.
   - Gateway to superconscious level of meditation.
   - There is a thin line of separation between the theta and delta brain waves.
   - Brain activity slows down to five to eight cps.

4. Delta brain waves:
   - This is the slowest brain wave.

- Brain activity goes down to 1.5 to four cps.
- This is the highest level of meditation; you are not dreaming and you are half awake.
- The brain releases unexplained substances, including human growth hormones, and increases endorphin levels, neuron transmission, the number of brain cells, adult stem cell function, and automatic repair mechanisms. The immune system becomes very powerful and protects us from opportunistic invading viruses, bacteria, and cancer cells, and destroys cancer cells (see pages xii–xiii).
- Our mind is so well organized at this superconscious level during meditation that it can project and determine the precise amount of purified grand ultimate chi energy that can heal, cure, or reverse and stop further growth of cancer cells.

You have learned the basic knowledge of self-healing, and upon this knowledge you will build a solid and strong foundation. Once you have reached your thousand-mile personal, professional, and spiritual journey and have reached the mountain top, you will find the true meaning of your existence. You will realize that there is nothing to fear of the unknown; for life is just a memory, and everything that happens in our life cycle happens for a reason, which we do not fully understand. The world and all its material contents will simply vanish in our minds. This knowledge of self-healing that we have learned will become our guiding light and a permanent companion for the rest of our lives.

Lastly, as we age and mature, we should be brave; we should accept and approach the end of our lives with dignity, happiness, and peace of mind. I believe that when our physical bodies die, our souls will not die. They will continue to live and bring us everlasting life, endless happiness, and peace of mind with our Lord Jesus Christ.

CHAPTER 7

Procedure for Self-healing Medical Chi Kung Meditation

There are three different positions you may assume during meditation:

1. Sitting on a sturdy, stable chair with both feet touching the ground. Both hands should rest on the thighs with the palms of both hands facing up. (A favorite for most people.)

2. Standing in a horse stance position with slightly bended knees, both hands extended forward, palms facing each other as if you were holding a large ball. (Difficult for most people.)

3. Sitting down on the floor in tai chi position. (This is difficult, especially for people with

vascular insufficiency problems, diabetes, peripheral neuritis, etc.)

The very first thing that you should do is to make a health plan of your own. Remember that this self-healing method is meant as secondary support management. Then, ask yourself, is this secondary support management the method that I should be using to help improve or heal my cancer and chronic illnesses? If your answer is yes, then go ahead and follow the instructions. If your answer is no, then you should not get involved with self-healing.

It is important to know that there is no quick solution or treatment to any medical problem. For beginners it will take sometime to store the grand ultimate purified internal chi energy. As a result, it is advisable not to heal your cancers and illnesses immediately. Your chi energy is still undeveloped and will take sometime to mature and become powerful. Have patience and your great effort will be rewarded.

Continue daily practice of accumulating your chi energy in the lower tan tien and perineal pouch. The more chi you pack snug and condensed in the lower tan tien and perineum, the stronger the chi becomes. It may take a month or more to mature and purify your chi energy. This will depend upon your strong personal commitment and your yi—intent and visualization. Your chi energy will let you know when you are ready to heal your illnesses and cancers. You will feel fullness, heaviness, pressure, or a tingling sensation in the lower tan tien area. Once you feel this heavy sensation, you can start projecting the chi energy to the intended target to heal your cancer or illness. Some practitioners can mature their chi energy in a few days or immediately. I wish you the best.

This is my recommendation for beginners:

First week of Chi Kung Meditation

This is the period of learning and is the most difficult part to do. You have to master concentration before using the chi energy. Begin with silence for thirty minutes, like an owl who is sitting on a branch in the quiet of the night, patiently waiting for his prey. The less he speaks, the more he hears; the more he hears the less he speaks. We can be like this wise owl and have the courage to develop patience and silence. Silence does not come easily; it takes self discipline to acquire.

Second week of Chi Kung Meditation

If you feel you are ready for the next step, start breathing and moving the chi energy exercise, guiding, moving, and storing the chi energy in the lower tan tien and perineal pouch. Remember: the continous radiant white yang chi energy (like lightsabers) and the black yin chi energy comes from heaven and enters the crown of your head. The black yin chi and the white yang chi energy comes from Earth and enters the plantar surface of both feet to the perineal pouch in the pubic region for storage. Do this exercise slowly, first with the white chi energy. When you feel some pressure and you are satisfied, then start the black yin chi energy storing in the perineal pouch. NOTE: Refer to steps 29 through 35 as a guide for the breathing and mind-moving chi energy exercise (conscious level). After you store the chi energy in both pouches, make sure to close both pouches to prevent chi energy from escaping. Open the pouches when you are going to store energy and close them when you are finished.

Third week of Chi Kung Meditation

By now, you will feel the chi energy building up in the lower tan tien and perineal area. You will feel heaviness, pressure, or a tingling sensation in the lower abdomen. This means that your chi energy is overflowing, maturing, and ready for healing the cancer. If you don't feel any heavy sensation yet, then continue Chi Kung meditation as suggested above for another week or more until you feel the chi energy pressure or heaviness. Once you are sure that the energy is ready, then proceed with the actual Chi Kung meditation as described below.

I – CONSCIOUS LEVEL

1. Find a peaceful place in your home—usually your room—and use this place every day.

2. Wear loose and comfortable clothing.

3. Have your usual light dinner. Wait about three to four hours after eating before you start Chi Kung meditation. It is advisable to meditate on an almost empty stomach.

4. Empty your bladder (urinate).

5. Try stretching exercises slowly for about three to five minutes to loosen up your muscles.

6. Go to the chosen meditation place.

7. Light one regular candle on a steady crystal holder or use a tea candle (precautionary measure to prevent fire).

8. Burn one to three sticks of incense on a fire-

proof holder (precautionary measure to prevent fire).

9. Play soft classical or easy-listening music that you like at a low volume you find comfortable.

10. I made it easy for you to remember two colors, namely white rays of continous yang radiant chi energy coming from heaven (similar to lightsabers) that enter the crown or vertex of the scalp, and the black yin chi energy that comes from the Earth and enters the plantar surface of both feet.

11. Choose one of the three positions I mentioned above. I prefer sitting down on a chair, both feet touching the ground without any effort or pressure. Knees are at a ninety-degree angle.

12. You and the chair should face east, as there is plenty of chi in this direction.

13. Relax all the muscles from the head down to the toes, with special attention to the muscles in the back of the neck and upper back. These muscles are hard to relax.

14. Palms of both hands face up on top of both thighs, resting comfortably without tension.

15. Put the tip of your tongue at the palate behind the front teeth. You can let go temporarily when you exhale during the breathing exercises.

16. Remove all the surrounding noises you can, and don't pay attention to the surrounding noises you cannot remove. Let the noise go.

17. Remove all negative thoughts and past negative memories.

18. Remove ego, anger, hatred, anxiety, and depression.

19. Forgive all those who have offended you.

20. Accept and love yourself the way you are, nothing less and nothing more.

21. Have a sincere outer and inner smile. Don't be shy, you are alone in the room.

22. Train the brain to cultivate positive thoughts.

23. Train the yi (intent and visualization).

24. You must have a strong conviction that you will be healed or cured.

25. In this stage of meditation, the beta brain wave activity is about fifteen to forty cps. You are fully awake, your mind is sharp and focused, and you have increased neuron transmission.

26. Open all the chi energy pathways and the seven chakras.

27. Close your mouth with the tip of the tongue touching the palate behind the front teeth.

28. Swallow clear watery saliva with plenty of chi energy.

29. Begin breathing exercises slowly and effortlessly.

30. Take a deep, long, and effortless breath with the abdominal type of breathing. Exhalation should be longer than inhalation.

31. Inhale through the nose with mouth closed; simultaneously expand or distend your stomach so diaphragm goes down. Do it slowly.

32. Exhale through the tiny opening in the center of the lips, at the same time contracting the stomach; the diaphragm goes up. Do not make any noise when exhaling. Do it slowly.

33. Immediately at the end of exhalation (breathe out), use the mind to guide the continous incoming yang white radiant chi energy and the black yin chi energy that slowly comes down from the heavenly connection. It enters the crown of your head and moves down to the base of the brain, to the spinal column, down to the second lumbar vertebrae of the back called the root chakra or what we call the Ming Men. Then the chi energy goes to the front to the lower tan tien where the white yang chi energy is deposited. After this, the black yin chi energy is deposited to the perineal pouch below. On the Earth chi energy pathway, the white yang and black yin chi energy enters the plantar surface of both feet, then goes up the back of the legs, thighs, pelvis, to the pubic region in the perineum. The white yang energy goes to the lower tan tien and the black yin energy goes to the perineal pouch for storage. Try to do the chi energy storage for the lower tan tien first, then the perineal pouch very slowly. Take all the time you want to concentrate on the chi energy moving.

34. Remember the yi (visualization and intention) for the transfer of yang and yin chi energies in their respective pouches. Again, some may not feel the chi energy immediately. Do not

get disappointed—you just have started the procedure.

35. When you feel heavy pressure or bloating in the lower abdomen, it means your pouches are filling up with chi energies. When you feel the pressure and the chi is overflowing, this means that the chi is ready for for mixing, condensing (packing snugly), and purification.

36. At this time, you may stop the breathing exercises; breathe normally without making a sound.

37. Now using the mind, open both lower tan tien and perineal pouches.

38. Guide the yang white radiant continously flowing chi energy down into the perineal pouch to be mixed, fully condensed (principle of condensation to fully packed snug chi energies) as soon as the yang and yin chi are mixed and condensed.

39. Using the mind again, guide these mixed yang and yin chi energies from the perineal pouch back into the headmaster lower tan tien for storage and purification.

40. Close both openings of the lower tan tien and perineal pouch.

II – SUBCONSCIOUS LEVEL

This is the level of deep thinking, with brain activity slowing down to nine to fourteen cps. Positive energy begins to flow. You are relaxed but not in a meditative state yet. It is a bridge to the superconscious level. There is a thin layer of separation between the theta brain wave, which is about five to eight cps, and the delta brain wave, at about 1.5 to four cps.

1. Now, with meaning and confidence, slowly and sincerely say the Lord's Prayer or whatever religious meditation prayers you are used to.

2. The powerful mixed yang and yin chi energy becomes transformed into a purified internal power. This internal power is now called the grand ultimate chi representing the perfectly balanced white and black tai chi symbol. This chi energy is very powerful, ready to be projected, and ready for treatment of the cancerous areas of the tissues or organs involved.

3. You will feel very relaxed and experience unexplained happiness and tranquility.

4. You may feel some goose bumps in the scalp and the upper and lower extremities. Some people who are used to deep meditation will feel as if the mind expands beyond the boundaries of their body, or as if they are floating in this vast, magnificent, beautiful, peaceful, and empty space in the universe.

5. This indivisible empty space is where God is.

6. God fills the entire universe. We may not see God; we may not touch God. God is a spirit and He is present everywhere. However, we can communicate with God or listen to what He is going to say to us. Our mind becomes like a blank CD that is ready to record what God is going to tell us.

7. You have now entered into a deeper level of meditation.

III – SUPERCONSCIOUS LEVEL

This stage of meditation includes the slowest brain wave activity, the delta brain wave; activity is 1.5 to four cps. This is the highest level of meditation for humans. You are still half awake, you are not dreaming, and you are in a completely tranquil state.

At this time, the brain releases the aforementioned unexplained substances, including human growth hormones; increased endorphins, neuron transmission, numbers of brain cells, and adult stem cell function and automatic repair mechanisms. The immune system becomes very strong and protects us from opportunistic invading viruses, bacteria, and cancer cells. It can destroy cancer cells, as we have discussed before. The mind is so well organized at this time that it can project and determine the precise amount of transformed and purified internal chi energy and power that can heal, cure, reverse, or stop the growth of cancers and progress of chronic illnesses.

1. Again using the mind, guide and open the headmaster lower tan tien pouch and begin projecting continously the grand ultimate chi energy going to the back at the Ming Men that either go upwards or downwards the spinal column, depending on where the cancerous tissue is you want to treat. For example, if your cancer is in the right lung, your mind guiding the powerful chi energy going upwards along the spinal column then goes to the right side of the lung. The powerful chi energy continuously pulverizes the cancerous area of the right lung, leaving alone the normal lung tissue. The pulverized, powdered

cancerous tissues turn into liquid, then into a gaseous state, and are expelled out through the pores in the skin. The rest of the cancer are expelled through exhalation.

2. Once the powerful internal grand ultimate chi energy touches the diseased or cancerous tissues or parts of the cancerous organs involved, only the cancerous portions will be pulverized into powder.

3. Subsequently, the pulverized cancerous tissues will be transformed into liquid, then into a gaseous state. The gas containing the bad chi will evaporate through the pores of the skin; the rest of the bad chi will be expelled through the lungs by exhalation.

4. I have no scientific clinical evidence to substantiate my theory. I will not be able to explain the miraculous process of self-healing, but healing does occur.

5. I may only say that this process of self-healing has helped many of my patients with faith, trust, positive thoughts, and belief in oneself and almighty God. Also it has helped me gain strength.

6. The final cleansing comes in. Imagine the continous radiant white ray of yang and black yin chi energy coming from heaven, going down into the crown of your head (heavenly pathway), replacing the remaining bad chi.

7. The mind is guiding the bad chi downward from the base of the brain down to the spinal column to the lower coccyx, pelvis, buttocks, back of the thighs, legs, and plantar surface of both feet down ten feet below the ground for permanent burial of the bad chi or cancer. The remaining good chi energy is retained in the lower tan tien and perineal pouch.

8. Remember this important note: After the healing has taken place, do not forget to close both lower tan tien and perineal pouches to prevent escape of precious chi energy. The more chi energy is stored, the more powerful your body will be.

9. Once you feel that healing has taken place, open both eyes, feel the stress suddenly relieved, and feel the peace of mind and happiness you have experienced.

10. You have now started achieving your goal in life through self-healing.

CHAPTER 8

At the End of Self-healing Medical Chi Kung Meditation

1. Continue Chi Kung meditation daily exercises at the same place, same time, if possible. Self-healing meditation should be done at least for one hour or more.

2. Your knowledge of self-healing will be your guiding light and become a permanent companion for the rest of your life. It will become your habit; it will become the values that will eventually lead to your own destiny. You have started achieving your purpose in life and have learned the true meaning of your existence here on planet Earth.

3. At the end of your successful self-healing

meditation, THANK GOD—the divine source, your own way, and your own method of praying. Say the Lord's Prayer with meaning, unhurriedly and attentively.

4. While you are still sitting down, stretch and wiggle or shake your upper and lower extremities all together for a few minutes to relieve muscle fatigue.

5. Move your neck very slowly to the right and left, up and down, slowly, to relieve muscle tension.

6. Massage the lower tan tien with the palms of both hands, left on top of the right hand; move the hands in circular motions thirty-two times counterclockwise, then thirty-two times clockwise.

7. Stand up slowly with help or while holding onto something strong like the chair to prevent dizziness and falling. Do stretching again for a few minutes, or do some slow treadmill exercise or walking.

I have written *Self-Healing Medical Chi Kung Meditation* to help my fellow human beings. It is available at wheatmark.com and amazon.com. This is the only book about self-healing that you will need to read because it is simple, easy to understand, complete, and effective, with illustrations that explain in complete detail how to do self-healing from the beginning to the end.

About the Author

Dr. Galvez completed his general surgery internship and residency from 1958 to 1965 at the following hospitals: Our Lady of Victory Hospital, Lackawanna, New York; All Saints Hospital, affiliated with Baylor University, Fort Worth, Texas; Sinai Hospital of Baltimore, affiliated with Johns Hopkins University Hospital; and Genesee Hospital in Rochester, New York, affiliated with Strong Memorial Medical Center and the University of Rochester School of Medicine and Dentistry, Rochester, New York. He started his private practice in 1965.

Dr. Galvez has been a member of the medical staff at El Camino Hospital in Mountain View, California, 94040, since April 1, 1975. If further assistance is needed, his email address is: e.g@sbcglobal.net. His website is: selfhealingchikung.com.

References

Baldock, John. *The Little Book of the Bible.* Rockport: Element Inc., 1993.

Chia, Mantak and Juan Li. *The Inner Structure of Taichi.* Huntington: Healing Tao Books, 1996.

De Maria, Frank. "Message from Grandmaster: We All Need Something, But What Is It." Croton on Hudson: American Center For Chinese Studies, 2005.

Dyer, Wayne W. *Wisdom of the Tao.* Carlsbad: Hay House, 2008.

Lam, Paul. *Tai Chi the 24 Forms.* New York: Wells Spring Media, Inc., 1999.

———. *Tai Chi the 32 Sword Forms.* Cordova: Fast Action video, 1996.

Liao, Waysun. *The Essence of T'ai Chi.* Boston: Shambhala Publications, Inc., 1995.

Peiqi, Xie. *The Eight Storing Qi and Developing Sen-*

sitivity Exercises of Yin Style Bagua. Hygiene: Association for Traditional Studies, 2004.

Pope John Paul II. *"The Way of Prayer."* New York: Crossroad Publishing Company, 2004.

Rinpoche, Sogyal. *Meditation.* New York: Harper Collins, 1994.

Sigman, Mike. *Exercises with Internal Strength.* Takoma Park: Plum Flower Press, 2004.

———. *Whole Body Movement with Internal Strength.* Takoma Park: Plum Flower Press, 2004.

———. *How to Do Internal Strength.* Takoma Park: Plum Flower Press, 2004.

Walters, Donald J. *Secrets of Meditation.* Nevada City: Crystal Clarity Publisher, 1997.

Winn, Michael. *Deep Healing Chi Kun.* Asheville: Healing Tao Home Study Video, 2000.

———. *Sexual Vitality Chi Kung.* Asheville: Healing Tao Home Study Video, 2001.

———. *Audio Five Animals Do the Six Healing Sounds, Qigong Fundamentals 1.* Asheville: Healing Tao Home Study Video, 2005.

———. Video *Five Animals Do the Six Healing Sounds Qigong Fundamentals 1.* Asheville: Healing Tao Home Study video 2004.

———. *Video Open the Microcosmic Orbit Qigong Fundamentals 2.* Asheville: Healing Tao home study audio, 2005.

———. *Video Open Chi Flow in the Orbit, Qigong*

Fundamentals 2. Asheville: Healing Tao Home Study Video, 2004.

Yogananda, Paramahansa. *Metaphysical Meditations*. Los Angeles: Self-Realization Fellowship, 1964.

———. *The Law of Success*. Los Angeles: Self Realization Fellowship, 1980.

———. *How You Can Talk with God*. Los Angeles: Self Realization Fellowship, 1985.

———. *Scientific Healing Affirmations*. Los Angeles: Self Realization Fellowship, 1990.

Additional References

Master Stephen Co gave a lecture, "Pranic Healing," in honor of the late Grand Master Choa Kok Sui, author of many Pranic healing books. The lecture was given on October 15, 2009, at East West Bookstore, 324 Castro Street, Mountain View, California 94040.

"Meaning of Colors" by Sobriety Stones is available at http://www. Sobriety stones.com.

"A Beneficial Qigong Exercise Program," "An Essential Guidance System for Chi," "Meditation Techniques, Postures, & Focus," "Yi Taps the Subconscious & Channels Chi," and "Meditate for Acuity, Healing, & Insight" are available at http://www.chikung-unlimited.com.

SelfGrowth.com is an online self-improvement encyclopedia.

"Brain Sync." Howell, Kelly. 2009. Brainsync.com

"Brain Activity during Meditation" Website Internet 2009

"Smart Brain Technologies" Website Internet 2009